THE   DENNY   POEMS   1985–1986

THE DENNY POEMS 1985–1986

STORMLINE PRESS URBANA ILLINOIS

International Standard Book Number: 0-935153-05-5

This book is published with funds provided by the Billee Murray Denny Poetry Award Foundation of Lincoln College. Special thanks are extended to Jack D. Nutt, Ed.D., President, Lincoln College, and to the following members of the Board of Trustees of Lincoln College:

Stormline Press, Inc., a non-profit service organization, publishes works of literary and artistic distinction. The press is pleased to serve as publisher of this fine collection of poems.

Stormline Press, Inc.
P. O. Box 593
Urbana, Illinois 61801

Manufactured in the United States of America.

Contents

Every year, the same contest is a little different — the content throws an altered light on the judging format we have developed over the last six years. Sometimes you remember the difficulty of choosing among the twenty or so poems that have made it through all the rounds to the top, judge after judge. All of them may have a great deal to offer, and all of them may have flaws that cannot be overlooked: a few mismanged line breaks, some ineffective punctuation, a spectacular image that goes nowhere and connects nothing, a plodding or rambling that leaks the energy right out of the lines. But sometimes, what you remember are the times you spotted a winner in the very first round, and then watched it inch its way to the top of a stack of 2400 others, round after round. After six years, what I have learned is that you can't keep a good poem down.

What makes a poem leap out of the stack of hundreds and announce itself a winner? Again and again, Valecia, Jim and I have discussed this. It has to do with magic, partly, a mesmerizing of the reader that occurs immediately, in the first lines, like a hypnotism replete with a post-hypnotic suggestion to insure the command is remembered. There is an authority of voice in the poem — something like Marge Piercy says commands her to write, "when all the voices become one voice." The voice of the poem says, no matter what else it may be saying, *I know whereof I speak, listen to me.* And there just isn't the possibility of not listening, for immediately a whole universe is announced and if two words, two lines are read, the reader is hooked by that world of the poem, where every sign is a marker that maps a geography as compelling and full of recognition as a trip back home through the best or worst moment of your own life. No matter what the subject matter or the place or characters in the poem, the poem says, *this is me and I am you.*

"Ice Storm" announced itself like this:

> I used to tell you
> how it built within me slowly
> and came upon me quickly
> and you would nod yes,
> yes, yes.
> I'd tell you again
> the same story
> the next day and you
> would understand — yes
> you knew the feeling.

There is a grace of movement and energy that runs back and forth like a cobra's head between the short lines, which are somehow exactly right for this poem. One knows one is going to get bitten. One even knows how, immediately, and when — because of that mysterious *it* in the second line (an indefinite word only a rank beginner or a pro would dare to use) that recalls the *ice storm* of the title to the internal weather of the speaker with never so much as a single expository phrase. All the convention flags go down in the reader's mind: this is a contemporary usage of extended metaphor at its best. The entire poem is a vehicle for its subject. It will line up like the two sides of an algebra equation, with the exact same sense of certain discovery, and the reader will solve for x, the complaint of the poem:

> I begged you
> to remember, Yes, you said, I
> shall, and did not.
> Till at last you were white
> and silent,
> torn by wind-blows, frozen
> in affirmations.
> And I cleared a space on the windowpane
> and yes, I said, yes,
> there he goes.

Perhaps it was the stunning visual imagery of "Windmills at Kinderdyck" that heralded a winner, imagery that becomes the metaphoric vehicle of the poem. The descriptions emblazon themselves on the inner eye, and at once the reader is there, sensing the alien familiarity that the powerful object-image of the huge Dutch windmills, with all the connotative resonance they have in terms of long-distance, non-verbal communication, gives to the scene of growing estrangement between the two, nation-crossed lovers:

> Here in the country, cows lower their legs
> into Dutch paintings, where yellow, anxious
> as a scream, settles on the Dutch daffodils,
> *fresia*, huddling low against the wind.

The image foregrounds the anxiety that rises throughout the poem; the color of yellow shocks the last stanza again, without even being mentioned except in the image that is its associate, daffodils:

> But I will get the weather wrong. All the while
> I am calling signs and portents, my hands trumpeting
> like daffodils, you will be stripping the windmills of power.

The third place poem of that year, "Sandhill Cranes, Platte River," has a longer, more narrative line. The skill of the poet shows in the turning from stanza to stanza. These turns develop situationally, with the same sense of impending betrayal and the likelihood of a self-fulfilling prophecy that the poem's subject matter is about. Even routine affairs of nature are implicated in the potential betrayal, and how much more ripe for this are human ones:

> It is that time in the cycle of things
> they are to return.
>
> Nothing is like it was: I am thinner
> in my belief in the routine progress of the seasons
> anymore, but we decide to drive the
>
> hundred miles west to find the Cranes. You
> are near to me as hope is to doubt, and, today
> as distant. I think we will find

nothing. I mistake
empty sky for them — too early, they
do not fly this far east — then I point at geese:
you say, "no, those are geese." Then I hear their voices
entangled in the blank and greying sky where they are not.

Again the resolution of the complaint comes poetically, through metaphoric expectation. The two searchers, abandoning their car, find a milkweed pod still closed from a summer before. Upon opening it, there are folded silks like "unfurled feathers" "still wet" — and the Cranes magically "move and call and fly" overhead. The tension here, weighed in a balance of hope and dread, is released utterly. Perfectly. All directions and contraries are resolved: up and down, going or staying, human betrayal and nature betrayal, human and natural restoration to faith in the general cycle of things. As fine a closure as I've read.

"Abandoned House," the winner for its year, moves slowly and deliberately through its strophic organization, stanzas camera ready in their visual clarity. There is nothing here that one cannot see, as though revealed in the visual detail will somehow be the invisible problem of why this house, this woman's way in the harsh male environment, is abandoned:

I pass foundations sunk deep in phlox
front steps climbing banks of purple vetch and
doorframes opening to wilderness. A path
perhaps to blueberries and the sea
and here and there, like offerings, simple ruins
of women's lives — wash tubs, a hand wringer,
the handle of a painted cup . . . .

It is not so much to understand that the persona returns to this place, but rather she returns like a criminal to the scene of the crime: she wants to be forgiven for a crime she had no choice but to commit in this male landscape made into home by lonely and long-suffering women; forgiven for her recognition that she could not play her tailored role. The problem is uncovered slowly through investigation and discovery through lost objects. Now that the mother's dead, her gifts can be prized. Yet there is no way to use the gifts. That world in which defined usefulness has died for lack of people. The last lines fulfill every expectation and need created in the poem:

Who will love this house
now she is gone?
The wind that rocks the raspberry hoops?
The mouse that sings to her young in the bread box?

"Fool for Love" is a *tour de force* of wit and rousing humor. (The judges wanted to take this poet out for a drink.) It begs to be read aloud, performed, hammed. Actually it is the ham in the persona's voice that utterly disarms the reader. This voice is for *real*. And this poem is absolutely different from the little gnomic poem "What is a Fiddle." This poem is symphonic in a country way, like a fiddle compared to a violin. The sound system harmonizes with a twang of assonance and alliteration. Richard Wilbur would love this poem, with its sure oscillation of tonal register from long *o*'s, to long *i*'s, to *e*'s. The judges fairly leaped at this poem. It is short (rare these days) and perfectly delightful in its final inversion, prepared for so very carefully in the rest of the poem. Somewhere in it there is a tight secret, locked. But the poem resists analysis, like any gnomic poem. It teases.

Once, early during last year's contest, there was a poem that I put immediately on the "no" pile as one of the worst poems I had ever read. The poem, however, had the vitality of a ghost whose body had suffered a violent death, and I became haunted. The next day, I exhumed it from the huge pile in which it lay buried and read it a few more times. It was either the worst or the best poem. I put it in the "maybe" stack to be sent on to the next judge. The poem's ghost didn't haunt that judge, for it got buried again. Still, I thought about it, obsessively, and so during the final round, I dug it out of the old stacks. Finally, the ghost turned out to be more powerful than the poem, and I buried it again, at last.

The experience of the margins of poetry, where great and hideous cross, is not unusual in a contest of this sort. Often, those poems that make it into the final anthology test in some way any assumption about good poetry one cares to make. One can assume, for example, nothing about the line, that old furrowed hallmark of a well-wrought poem. Contemporary poems make up their own rules. The good ones follow them. Sometimes the bad ones make up their own rules and follow them too. Sometimes you need the judgement of several people to tell the difference. Poetry has its own perversities. In this anthology of winners, there is a great deal to discover and delight in, very little to quibble with.

Lucia Cordell Getsi

Ice Storm

I used to tell you
how it built within me slowly
and came upon me quickly
and you would nod yes,
yes, yes.
And I'd tell you again
the same story
the next day and you
would understand — yes,
you knew the feeling.
I told you a year later
and you took the tale
into your heart, your dream, and
yes, that is
how it goes,
you said, once
again.
And even as I spoke,
and you spoke,
the edge of my lung turned silver,
and the air I breathed out
imperceptibly fragile
as you kissed it; yes,
you said, yes: we
will keep warm.
I told you the shaking began
in the trees
and only the birds
could feel it. Birds,
you'd repeated, nearly
sleeping.
I let you see my nails
where the lavender began,
and you took my hands
and yes, you said,
it would be fearsome,
what a tragedy is nature.
I said you were unprotected,
but you walked without thinking.
Again and again
I gave you warm clothes,
I begged you
to remember. Yes, you said, I
shall, and did not.
Till at last you were white
and silent,

13

torn by wind-blows, frozen
in affirmations.
And I cleared a space on the windowpane
and yes, I said, yes,
there he goes.

Windmills at Kinderdyck

> *At this canal in the twelfth*
> *century, windmills were used*
> *at floodtime for communication.*
> *Millers signalled events to*
> *neighbors across the waters*
> *by turning blades.*

Beneath the chill air of flatlands, we ride
along the Kinderdyck, canal of your childhood.
Here in the country, cows lower their legs
into Dutch paintings, where yellow, anxious
as a scream, settles on the Dutch daffodils,
fresia, huddling low against the wind.
We ride close to the black water.
I am shuddering in your Dutch summer.
You teach me to say: The sun is shining:
De zon schÿnt! I chant like a spell.
But the flowers grow sick of rain. You tell me I am:
een van de bloemen. I repeat: one of the flowers.
But my sea-logged hands listen for more.

On either shore survive these ancient windmills,
signals of the soul's weather in time of flood —
a winged speech:
not so open, closed today
birth in progress, death downwind.
Events are easy to confuse: tongues cross,
and the chained halfmast of friendship looks like love.
Fans draining the fields slip into lock then start up
quickly with the first breeze to slice a man in two.
You turn away from me in the boat, your ice blue eyes
fixed on the lone egret splashing in the shallows.
You have skated again into your own world of frozen
water, some Hans Brinker fairy tale with birds.

Your sun comes out for one moment; your frown breaks
into a smile and you make light: People say I am Swedish,
and belong in some Bergman movie about dark glass.
I nod to myself: *I told you that. Touch me.*
I try to imagine living in your windmill, spending
my Holland moored on your canal, dodging blades
from some reedy silo, charting cycles of the rain,
changing signals from some tiny window like sails.
But I will get the weather wrong. All the while
I am calling signs and portents, my hands trumpeting
like daffodils, you will be stripping the windmills
of power. Soon we will sit there in silent watch: no
blades will turn over the land, no windmills flower.

Sandhill Cranes, Platte River.

I.
It is that time in the cycle of things
they are to return.

Nothing is like it was: I am thinner
in my belief in the routine progress of seasons
anymore, but we decide to drive the

hundred miles west to find the Cranes. You
are near to me as hope is to doubt, and, today,
as distant. I think we will find

nothing. I mistake
empty sky for them — too early, they
do not fly this far east — then, I point at geese:
you say, "no, those are geese". Then I hear their voices
entangled in the blank and greying sky where they are not.

Then, I see no evidence of them anywhere. A ten-thousand year
pattern broken: they are not here this year, I think.
Haltingly, I anyway assemble what I know of their past

migration, tell you they be red-headed,
coo something like distant pigeons. Simple
blocks, I say, from where we live, the zoo had one
we could have found, we could have seen.

II.
We drive the brown-grey roads platted into mile blocks
despite this river; we can find no road that runs with
it. We drive and drive, criss-crossing the river, oh, twenty

times or more. I am convinced we will find nothing, that we are
here for no reason we can name. We leave

the car as if it, too, has betrayed us, crouch through thickets,
over unused wire fences, trample years of weeds and nests and leaves.

A milkweed pod still closed from a Spring ago surprises us
to open it as if such a thing had not before ever
been discovered. Thumb to thumb, you pry apart along the seam.
Still wet inside lie folded silks like unfurled feathers.

Upstream a thousand feet, the Cranes —
they move and call and fly.

Honorable Mention Winners 1985

Margaret Benbow

Dream Of the Perfect Beast

A rank stranger appears in all my dreams.
His pigjaw rests on wolf sables
but in his lapel is a baby rose
and I am wearing a veil, a pouf of illusion.
Beneath it, my hair hobbles my knees,
great leashes of Victorian bridal hair.
My shoes are white kid, and I leap —
No. I can't move a muscle.
What a hungry little bride, starving all her life.
What a voice, luxury chocolate, busthead whiskey,
made for bold-faced lies and unspeakable confessions.
He stands so close
I'm afraid he's going to eat my face.
My yummy little bride, glazed like a bonbon
in pink and white and just made
to nestle in my hand, I see his fat voluptuous paw,
to be rolled under the tongue —

Even under bedsteads of sleep I tell myself
he arises from supper's stink cheese, a piece of gristle.
I invoke the name
of my daughter, EDEN,
but the flowery blast that buckles my neck
leaves him standing on legs like strong snakes.
"I will never, never put my hand
in the wolf's mouth," but my mind twists
like addled rabbit brains. His gaze sharpens.
Poor sweet! Though I terrify you to the hucklebones,
don't you know there are worse than I?
For the devil roams.
"I will kill you all, shoot shoot bang bang!"
But aren't you afraid of catching on fire?
"No." Yes, I am afraid of catching on fire.

I look for someone to save me,
a great Mama in a print apron
but armed with claws, tire irons, choppers.
Oh, she'll jump him,
she'll slam him about the head like a drunk
and count his bones. To her
I murmur "I'll be good!" and to him, "You dirty beast!"
He puts on his black gloves precisely
and smiles as though too polite to laugh.
Life will teach you to treat your obsessions
with a little more respect.

At the door he turns and says, *My heart —*
and I clap my hands over my breast
to keep it from leaping out.

Robert Crum

The Hereford

The smoke of dying fires rises
from the orchard, thinning the moon
until its reflection fills the cowpond
where a brown and white Hereford,
earlier that evening, wandering
off shore and sinking its hooves
in the cool, thick mud,
got stuck. It's out there now,
still lowing, baffled
but calm, like some dutiful god
of all domestic animals.
The swallows are gone
that for an hour flew circles
above its head, and in the pasture
the fireflies come on;
a sunfish leaps for one
just beyond the Hereford's tail.
Anyone leaving the orchard now,
tired and hungry after having pruned
the ranked, stubby trees all day,
and trying to decide whether to eat first
or sleep, would think nothing
about that bawling from the bottom-land.
But no one is leaving the orchard.
No one is opening the door
of the dark house. No one
sinks back into the overstuffed armchair,
his shoes still on.
And the night passes into the night.
The cricket panics before the mouse,
the mouse before the owl,
and the owl inside the pole-trap
the farmer set the night before.
All of which leaves the Hereford
unconcerned. All of which leaves the Hereford,
in fact, asleep. Never safer than now
with its knees locked in mud,
it nods its large head, and the rings of water
roll away from its nose all night.
All night the smoke and the moonlight
fall like the fabric of a dream
over the open land. And the mist rises
and thickens around the cow,
who will awaken inside this local cloud
watching the white distortions of its face
growing slowly clearer in the star-abandoned air,
floating there before it
over the imponderable water.

Catalogue

"Simple are the ways we come apart."
— Broadway musical *Nine*

One is a wishbone
licked clean.
Pulled from each side
tender tender
she snaps in two
unequal parts,
limps the rest of
her days away,
white and brittle as bone.

One suddenly empty morning
another, sealed for years
in sausage casing,
slides out of her skin.
She lands red
and meaty on the fine china.
They breakfast over her
mumbling how well she's
held up, considering.

A row of angora soft
and baby blue
unwinds quietly
in the corner.
No one hears
her woolen voice
rubbing against the knitting
basket, unraveling
stitch by stitch.

Helen Ellis

Leaning Back

Most often when I think of you, you're little:

A child beneath the branches of an apple tree
That's gnarled and well past apple bearing.
It's early summer and the grass and tree are green
Except that there are blossoms still, and so, belated
White. Your hair is yellow. And you wear
A short dark dress that could be blue, with lace
And ankle socks, and matching ribbons that pull
Your hair back from your face. The wispy strands
Get in your eyes, though, and you're squinting.
You have one arm around the tree, as if to hug it.
You were four then.

Or — when you're bigger, maybe six or seven,
I see you in a house, sitting by a table.
The wall and rug are orange and your legs,
Stuck out in front of you for close inspection,
Are red-splotched. Mother dabs white liquid
On them while you grimace, and she's crooning.
A bowl of berries, red and wet from rinsing,
Sits upon the table. You have one in your hand.
I watch you eat it.

Or — when you are eleven and your hair falls
To your waist, I see you standing just beside
A doorway that enters to the parlor. It is light
Behind you, dark before. And your body, rigid,
Leans a little backward to the light.
The sunlight makes the gold strands of your hair
Glint to silver. I cannot see your face
Although I am inside, in the parlor, where our mother
Lies, white as the apple blossoms on the tree.
But long past bearing.

Most often when I think of you, you're little —

But that's not always so. I think of you
A woman — still the hair that's yellow
But darker gold, like coins dug up from secret
Treasure buried deep inside a box long years ago;
Still the truth of squint and grimace and of the face
Kept hidden by the brightness of the sun; still
The hand that reaches out to take the berry,
and to hug the apple tree, and still the leaning
Back into the light before that firm step taken
Into the dark before.

22

Barbara Horton

When I Stand Looking At My Sleeping Child

the streetlight entering, slanting on
a patch of wood floor
there is a pause that hangs in the universe
I could be a she-bear — that massively close to the earth.
There is nothing she does not know as she lifts
a spangled fish from the ice and feeds.
She is of the earth, the ice, the planets revolving

the diurnal turning, the getting up and lying down
the sucking. I understand because my daughter sleeps
the breath and the blood, the blue, translucent lids.
The room's alive and pulsing. A tree
could grow here thick as centuries of endings and beginnings.
I am bending now
fertile as grass, brushing the sweet silk of her hair.

She is the core of the apple, the seed, the petal
the nectar, the sex, the light on the floor
a finger-prick of blood.
My footsteps echo. Outside
the white iced yard could last forever like a photograph —
Grandmother Williams lifting a hen from its nest
holding in her speckled hand the still warm egg.

Cynthia Huntington

What the Weatherman Said

"This is not the beginning of the Ice Age.
This is January." Though tonight heavy snows
bury Colorado and children are lost
on the Plains where a school bus drifts empty
on an empty road and small figures wander miles
past help, the storm will find us
in Massachusetts, forewarned and unafraid.

Ice quiets the singing Mississippi, and Illinois
goes dark a hundred miles across.
In the North Atlantic sea ice increases
each year, while prevailing winds change, wild
on the land, snapping power lines and shattering
barns into rubble of lumber. Still, we know
the extreme is not always abnormal.

Meanwhile the couple upstairs
are discussing their future in screams
above the sound of gunfire in Detroit
and she recommends he remove himself directly
to hell. I hear a fist slam wood,
the girl's sharp cry, and I think
they are not even real. They are abnormal.

What is real is the film they show later
of the shy rhinoceros shot down by tranquilizer
darts; crumbling into his skin, huge knees
breaking, he goes down and they drag him
into the truck and take him to a sanctuary
for the endangered, the nearly extinct,
where he eats so delicately whole branches of pine.

It is a fact the world has gotten too dangerous
for animals. But not for us!
And though tonight the hundred disasters
are broadcast, and families stand stunned
beside burned houses — their stored-up lives
they thought belonged in a box —
though tomorrow's murderer is waiting to confess

and will not be believed, we will sleep
assured of reports, warnings from the world we know.
The Great Lakes are frozen hard now
and across the Adirondacks a light snow
begins covering the fir and spruce, white on the edges,
dark beneath. In a small poor country my sleep
is being made safe by men with guns.

Tonight someone is being beaten to make me safe;
some small poor person has a dangerous idea; he wants
another life. He will not appear tonight;
he is nearly extinct; he is going away.
Now the storm is with him, walking
before him, and now the various animals who die
and are buried in ice, consumed

in the time of continents, before roads begin
or names of cities. The land changes now; just so
we will change without knowing
into another creature. And though the snow in Colorado
is immeasurable, filling each valley, moving east
toward us, this is not the beginning
as it is not the end. This is January, Massachusetts.
There is still time.

Mary (Chris) Leche

The Hunter

for Carolyn

Under the pool of sky
the duck's breasts open.
Again again the shot is good.
Father carries them home, feet
tied, bodies launched over one shoulder.
Heads lap the air like lost tongues of bells.
Beaks hit the tile counter with plastic knocks.
Two holes round as needle's eyes let air
in the orange mouths before the sun came up.
Your father waited in a blind. Now
he pops the top from a can of beer,
spreads a fan of mallard wing out
over the hollow bowl of kitchen sink,
plucks a purple feather for your hair.

And you heard how it was to field-dress
the deer, to warm stiff hands in a wet belly,
to pull the cradled entrails up, then leave
a mound of slop in the woods.
But you see it only hung from a beam of pine
out back. Father runs slits down the insides
of legs and thighs, the skin strips in sheets,
falls in a pile like wallpaper.
The deer's back arches with its own weight,
toes point, eyes like bowls empty to the still ground.

The elm empties too by November,
this first month blood drops down your thighs.
Mother says nothing, nothing, the way
blood runs from a girl.
Cool blood on your fingers.
Your father treats you differently.
He has learned the power of blood,
has turned it cold so often.
A slip of membrane like cellophane
holds the hide and meat of the deer tight.
The sound it takes to pull them apart
fills your abdomen. You cannot sleep.
In the dark, blood drips from the deer's nostrils.

Now you cut the woman's belly,
lift the tiny body with trained hands.

In another room, you order bottles
of blood to keep the old man warm.
Your father gave you this, a will
to save hot blood from going cold.

You want to tell them it's the same,
dying and dead we smell like the deer,
or duck parts tossed away.
And nothing stops it, this flow
falling from you.
You know it. You touch it.

Aunt Minnie And The Furies

Beyond the bay window the birds
are stranded in the scriptural air
and trees siphon cats
from the apple-skulled grass.
"There's no rest for the weary,"
she said, yanking on work gloves
and rocking a straw hat down
around her head, bending her ears.
The watermelon rinds wallow
in the bucket as far as the fence,
the chickens stand in line
until her back is turned.
Both she and the windmill
lisp through lost teeth.

The dog drags a shadow across
the hieroglyphic hollowings
of tractor tires, stops to sniff
the ruins of the pump shed,
the quilt of old wood
and scrap metal that buckled
in a blizzard and fell.
"Henry scrimped on nails,"
she said, kicking a loose board.
"I have a barrel of saved nails
in the cellar. Henry is gone."
Through blood-steep blossoms
of rust the red ants travel
the shed's twisted tin.

The sun-flesh doilies smolder
on heavy furniture,
ashes of austerities
like the pressed flowers
in the scrapbook, the special
plates in the cupboard.
"If wishes were horses,
beggars would ride,"
she said, brushing the web
of children's hands
away from the cookie jar.
The skeletal hour bargains
with the radio's static,
the beet tops in the sink.

The neighbors rent the fields,
except for the narrow strip
south of the creek. Just weeds.
Henry had made that field first.
Far enough from the house

to sing the songs learned
in the navy, he chased trees back
to the creek, laid the snake across
the new fence like an altar cloth.
"At noon I walked out
with another water jug
and sandwiches," she said.
"We sat in the shade and divided
up the silence evenly."

When the child's illness
brought the corners of the room
together and strangers stood
in pools of prayers, she shooed
dust off the sullen toys
and fed the flowers to the hogs.
"No one dies until we get
the garden in," she said, shuffling
the thin deck and bending
the corner of the Old Maid card.
In the attic now, condemned
to unfamiliar names, the alphabet
blocks stall for time, vines paw
the windows and mumble passwords.

Grinning like a drowned sailor,
the tangled clothes drift
in the tub's gray water.
Rows of birds watch
from blistered branches.
The bare ground braces itself
for the greasy water.
"The denim wouldn't dare fade,"
she said, her knuckles galloping
across the washboard.
Going mad in the moonlight,
the clothespins chew
through the thin ropes
and wander off with the wind.

The last lightning trickles
out of the sky, the rain has ended,
clouds are spread out
like documents in a museum,
setting an example
for the new mushrooms,
the white dragons
drunk with darkness, lifting,
blinking, in the strange
sprawl of the sun.
"They never see me coming,"
she said, pulling the butcher knife
out of her basket.
"I get them from behind."

Lillian Robinson

Poetics Five

for Kolker

That heat-wave when Delmore Schwartz died, Bob and I
called and the funeral folks told us no one
had taken charge. Well, we were in our mid-
twenties, but young for our age, because earnest
pursuit of the doctorate does maintain
the state of innocence over-ripe,
but we wanted to get Delmore out of there
and make a ceremony of decent,
soft farewell. Bob and I were in fifth grade together
and here we were teaching
Columbia sophomores and living our real
life at the movies. I hadn't written
a poem in years and now I'd come down
with dissertation block, as well, but Bob
was writing his about Blake, so didn't.
The body of the poet, rotting fast,
like Zossima's all too human, waited
for the stench to override the vapor
of exasperation he'd trailed behind him
all his days. We felt it was our duty
to claim it in default of intimates.
Hilarious and mourning, 'We've got to get
Delmore out of there.' We had no money,
no right, and 'We're a couple of grad students,
Bob, I reminded him, 'little *pischers*,'
and everyone knows grad students can't do
anything. I should have claimed that body
as a *poet*. Fighting mortality
with the doubtful adequacy of words,
we've all earned that much from our fellows:
'I demand this corpse in the name of writing,
if not of Literature. We will take care
of it, give it proper burial and see
to the resurrection in good time. Find
me a shovel, Bob (I should have ordered),
I'm going down to Campbell's in my mini-
skirt to stop this nonsense, break my writer's block.'
Later, they called that time the Summer of Love.

Lillian Robinson

Sonny Ghost

> *Your child will play the role*
> *of Sonny Ghost, a shy little*
> *pillow slip.*
>> — Note sent
>> home from
>> Synergy School,
>> San Francisco,
>> October 1983

I
My voice, they always told me, *carried* so well
without shouting; it could lift a gradeschool
production right off its stumbling blocks and up
into (if not the empyrean) at least
lucidity. I was the announcer,
always, the explainer. Even though I learned
everyone else's part before they did
that merely meant I could memorize,
never perform. Perhaps they thought no one
would trust me in character, so insistently
myself as I was. Maybe it's the standard
for a bespectacled, wildhaired, skinny kid
who can't even carry a tune but bears
enchanted speech in her far too often sore throat.
That school burned down, its ruins (I swear it)
are now a fire station. Arson it was
but I, a doctoral student, by then,
was innocent, the only flame I tend
that implacable torch in my body
always lit up, aching to get on stage.

II
Children are not the ghosts of our intentions
nor the embodiment of our projects.
Lady, my son might address me, like a cabbie
refusing some exotic destination
way off his meter, *I've got no time to live*
back your unhappy childhood for you. No one
can ever get reimbursed for that. (What if
my father came back who died when I was 4?
See? Not even a miracle would suffice!)
My Mozart, my Galileo, my Stuart
Mill, my skinny baserunner, my circus
tumbler, tote your own banners in this bizarre
parade; it doesn't lighten my burden
one feathersweight to make you share it too.

III
Write about the Universal Universe,
commands the sign in my dream. But I'm obsessed
with particulars: my son's eye ringed with black
ghost-shadow and the jaunty swing of his sheet.
A revenant from our family pan-
demonium has shown up in the flesh
to help with his costume. This nightmare is real,
while my notion that his imaginary
10 foot-tall brother and sister are the ghosts
of my two abortions — *that* is fantasy.
No stage fright, but: *I'm supposed to say 'Boo!'*
timidly and I'm afraid if I'm timid
no one will hear me! On any boards you tread,
remember your mother's voice will carry
you out of her own mourning memories,
where it's always the day of my specific dead,
into anywhere in this century
or next that's worth the penetration.

Peter Sears

Night Golf

We tee off under the moon
and walk into my first hole of Night Golf.
My ball is nowhere. I drop another ball
and send a seam along the dark.
This ball I lose too. I like the swat,
the moon night tingling, but I will lose
no more balls. I pretend, I swing
on a ball I imagine. My friends stroll over
and say I am picking up the game fast.
Thanks loads, I reply. At the top of my backswing
I see myself naked. I laugh,
go to my knees. My friends laugh with me.
I try again, I swing without a club
and walk under the ball
I see floating to the green. There,
I stroke a long putt, my head down
over my followthrough. I don't keep score.
There is no score in Night Golf.
You swing and look your ball into the dark.
You walk with friends across land you don't know,
saying little, allowing your stride
to find a softness you vaguely recall.
You may go far with yourself,
far, and be content by morning.
If not, the day floats
beyond your envisioning of the moon rising
and your teeing up again.

Barbara Winder

The Destroying Angel

> *Henry James, Senior, told his daughter, Alice,*
> *that she could end her life whenever it pleased her,*
> *but that she should "do it in a perfectly gentle*
> *way in order not to disturb her friends."*

She might go out into the garden behind their
house, sit for a while on the bench that her
brother, William, had painted for her, watch
the jays fighting for their territory,
dispersing the wrens who disappear under
cover of juniper; she might glance toward
the house to be sure no one was watching, and
then, with bird cries still tearing the air,
she might just stop breathing.

Or, after a performance of chamber music,
she might return home and play at the piano
for a while; Schumann would be appropriate;
she has read how he suffered all his life
from "a mortal anguish of mind." One day, .
he threw himself into the Rhine, but was
rescued by boatmen who saw a figure dressed
in black plunge off a bridge in an arc
of darkness. When the piece is done, she
feels the tears. The composer said that
one can die of sadness.

Her father would approve of her walk in the woods.
She holds the book in her hand, studying the diagram
of *Aminita Phalloides*, the Destroying Angel.
The mushrooms under her feet are edible, but
there is time. If Alice is successful, she
will eat them here, under these pines. A breeze
rises in the early evening air, and the girl
shivers. In the failing light, she reads
that one bite will suffice, and she kneels to
examine a flattened pileus. She thinks if she
is lucky, she will recline beside the pond
beyond this copse, her head resting on a stone.
When they find her, no one will be disturbed
because the hill is mirrored in the lake, birches
bend over it as if to take a sip, and her face
will be a cameo in the growing light.

Abandoned House

I
I pass foundations sunk deep in phlox,
front steps climbing banks of purple vetch and
doorframes opening to wilderness. A path
perhaps to blueberries and the sea
and here and there, like offerings, simple ruins
of women's lives — wash tubs, a hand wringer,
the handle of a painted cup.

This is the lonely dunescape
where sand swells and seeps like water,
where beach pea and wild roses leisurely plunder,
giving up flowers and fruit for no one.

I return searching
empty rooms
where all that holds
holds as if by will,
weathered boards and
pine tree bones
scoured to a fine patina,
an assault so slow
it resembles lovemaking.

Domain of women, slow oven,
mind's casket, goddess I fear,
I am the fugitive who comes back
trying to understand
what happened here.

II
The sand path rises steeply — a sudden glimpse
of sea on my right and ahead, Balston Heights
and the abandoned house — graceful porch with
spindled balustrades, many rooms. Beyond,
the sea that whales still frequent.

Against male gods of shipwreck
and heavy catch, these women
sank their households in the cliff head,
hung white curtains at the windows,
softening what they could,
lowered buckets into shallow wells.

A rabbit trembles on the path as I approach,
waits, its eye upon me, bolts into the under-
brush, all reflex and speed.

I didn't choose. I bolted
like a small animal whose spine
is a hot wire signalling
danger. I fled my mother and
her mother before her, their lives
as I saw them twisted in sacrifice.
I saw them lean toward others
like flowers toward the sun
and I said no.

A mourning dove sounds her five sad notes.
I hear in her obsessive music
all I've lost.

III
Mother, tell me again all will be well,
that the family will gather this time without bitterness,
the drunkard not rise up to beat the children,
the butchers lay down their knives and worship animals,
the makers of warheads dance out their darkness.
Mother, tell me again all will be well
if I but lay the table generously,
keep the house,
bear children.

I lean my forehead against the porch rail.
At my feet, blueberries gleam,
little heirlooms
flung in the grass.

IV
I push against the rusted latch
and enter with the ease of kin,
trying to catch some scrap of wholeness.
I come for comfort or forgiveness
as if to the grave of a tyrant
mother whose gifts —
now she is dead — I can prize,
her once-prim lilies vaulting the fence,
her lilacs wild in the field.
Who will love this house
now she is gone?
The wind that rocks the raspberry hoops?
The mouse that sings to her young in the bread box?

Fool For Love

to a friend

He wrote haikus to "her delicate Victorian silences,
her little geisha feet." He meant me, and never knew
I hissed *Mistaken identity*, mentally swung hagfish
and heaved them in his face, kicked him with doll's feet
and slapped him silly.
I always wanted to be like the wild women in old movies
who have whole storm systems of black hair,
who are earthy and hotten things up
and whose great talent is in letting themselves
go, go, go. (Oh, let it be me,
Dolores del Rio in *Bird of Paradise*
when with star-shaped tears and not one word
she slowly chews the pomegranate,
then puts her lips to the feverish lips of Joel McCrea
and passes the fruit into his mouth: a last look:
then goes away, doomed, gorgeous,
to throw herself into the volcano.)

Young men in old movies are fools for love.
Heathcliff smashes his fist through glass.
King Kong's eyes run rivers as Fay Wray
sits in his hand for the last time.
John Garfield rides beside Ann Sheridan in a dusty coupe,
looks her up and down, "I'm crazy about yah, baby,"
and lustily cracks his gum.
Then, too, there is Valentino advancing
with rich Latino menace, through fogs of patchouli,
toward that woolly lamb Agnes Ayres:
"Why — why have you brought me here?"
He narrows his eyes and wonderfully replies,
"Mon Dieu! Are you not woman enough
to know?"

Fumbling among perfumes, I choose Tabu.
In the ad, it is clear the man and woman (in evening dress)
have been playing some noble ravishing phrase from Beethoven
and now his hands crush her strapping shoulders,
her neck rears like a pulsing snake.

I quote Mick Jagger to myself,
and then Camus:
It's all right to let yourself go
if you can get yourself back.

Sometimes to suppress a dive
leaves one strangely aching.

All around me the high flyers plummet past.
The neighbor girl colors her grand fall
with severe strokes of black and white,
"Friday night I went out for cigarettes, met Chad,
Monday morning I woke up on Pine Island —
oh, God, it's all a blank."
She draws on a cigarette, leaving me
to envious surmise.
Her irises range around, pure goofball
and yet marbled with lovely colors from the moon
and from Pine Island,
drugged lilac, blackest thorn.

I curse my little geisha feet
that never climbed a diving board.
Furiously I revise my script,
adjust for age and climate, determined that someday
I too shall have my splashy steamy plunge.

When I am an old burning loaf of a woman
(perhaps in Europe, where ripeness is all)
I will look into the eyes of some hairy attendant
who makes my bed, and counts my bones.
He will measure out my nitroglycerine,
give me little sips. "Are you comfortable?"
I'll ignore him, smell a rose. He'll say,
"What more can I do?" At last:
I'll give him a *film noir* look and hiss,
"Mon Dieu, are you not man enough to know?
Read my lips."

What Is A Fiddle

A fiddle is a violin played
out of doors, a handmade song composed
of pine, maple, sycamore, joined
to a player's curved throat, scrolled arms,
in harmony with the long-eared owl's
one note. In the pauses, a proximate quiet:
bluegills ripple, oarlocks at dockside reply.
With ordered delight, the fiddler and the fiddle's
turned woods raise up the voice of the rooted.
The wind rehearses trees for this.

Honorable Mention Winners 1986

Charles Atkinson

First of Fall, with Thunderheads

You've left the chidren at school,
their first ecstatic day, and drive back
too fast, knowing you should be more careful
and unwilling to try — hoping to outrun
the clouds, and what waits when you're alone.
Something you've avoided these last weeks
with the quick of living muted by heat
and sleep and the drone of children's needs,
with all fibers grown amber
and turned from self-knowing.

In so much dust and glare
you've forgotten how to find yourself
awake within rain's small perfections —
the weathered fence alert with moss,
the madrone's bare, shining thigh —
and how to listen at a beaded window
to the thoughtful ear speaking to itself.
Each time you've forgotten, another drop
has dried in the pool, the self's bowl
set in earth, unpunctured by yes and no.

Now smell it — season's first
rusty nitrous storm, its hard drip-drop
insisting — *here* you are, how could you
neglect the nearest pulse, the leaves aflame?
You're on the exit ramp, still too fast,
when the big drops splash, knowing
what to expect when you slow: sheets of it,
weeks, until you wake fully on a fall night,
as if in rising water, knowing — time is short,
can I rouse even my own children?

Melissa Cannon

Breaking

I'm washing dishes when your shrill ring breaks
the quiet drift of clouds and I'm called back
to daylight where dust scatters misty smoke
around the room. The phone slides in my hand;
it smells like wax-clogged rags and soured cloth.
You're breathless, taut, half-halting as you give

me the bad news: the cups I searched to give
you so we'd have a pair — one's smashed. Fear breaks
along my spine until my skin's soaked cloth.
You've asked if it's a sign. Oh, take it back —
what silliness, to talk as if your hand
were that of fate. But the words burn into smoke.

Such ghostly words infiltrate us like smoke.
My teacher Ev, for whom I ached to give
love gifts, embarrassments, books made by hand,
joked at my raw adolescent heartbreaks,
said some love scared her, so I put it back
unused as draped chairs buried under cloth.

Your mother wore away like thinning cloth.
After she died, you said, "She's less than smoke,"
air vanishing that nothing could bring back.
Two years — I think she's still alive. I'd give
the world to comfort you when that pain breaks
out of your throat, a startled bird: my hand

can only smooth your back or grip your hand
while her words envelop you in mourning cloth.
I last saw Ev on one of her school breaks;
she laughed her laugh of coffee and stale smoke
and said I'd better call. She made me give
my word: "Or if I die, I'll sure come back

to haunt you." And she died, flat on her back
in the teachers' lounge — a burst vein closed her hand.
I sort through words for an image we could give
our lives — we're threads and crossthreads, woven cloth,
not thin-stemmed glassware or dissolving smoke.
I want to tell you "Love —," but my voice breaks.

And hers seeps back: low, filtered through rough cloth;
with her shaking hand still itching for a smoke,
she says, "Don't give me anything that breaks."

Regina deCormier-Shekerjian

January 1

The wind, this morning,
runs just out of reach of the chipped teeth
of the sea, a red shout cutting a hole
in the sky above the kitchen where
a kettle mutters its slow speech of fish heads
and bones . . . .
                    Here,
on the coast, even those nights we wake
to the thunder of moonlight, morning
is there, with its eye to the chink,
to remind us our days are plotted by the sea's
mathematician, the master of zero,
the plain speaker.
In this season he courts the boreal wind
with a hail of curses and shrieking
gulls ride the wind like witches,

while we shunt and burrow through the long night
of winter with the Reverend Owen Jenkins
talking of blessings, lipreading the weather,
and pushing a buggy full of bad dreams
down the aisle out into the snow-withered street
where his customary Sunday sermon
lies buried. It is

six months

since the Rugosa was in bloom,
and my child, born irreparably defective, was
buried — yes, like all the so-called runts
of the town's litters — buried
in the back yard.
There's no use pretending. The truth
of our ghosts is here, under the thin blanket
of soil on this granite coast where the sea
gnaws, and ravels its gossip,
and drums the seasons around the hoop
of the year. This morning

when a thin blade of light knifed
the black sky from the black sea, I watched
the men go out to sea. From the window
I watched their lights move
toward the horizon.

The wind had not yet risen.

Beethoven's "Rage Over a Lost Penny"
singed the edges of silence.

from *Letters from the Coast*

Regina deCormier-Shekerjian

May 30

In this town of straight talkers
everyone said young Tad Jamison was honest
to call himself a snake-oil salesman.
A newcomer, he peddled his shrimp and his charms
with a fabulist's tongue, traded mysteries for cash
and secrets for supper while fast-talking
the minister into believing him blessed by the angels
in broken shoes. He said he was a shaman
hatched from an egg in a linden tree, said he was
one of the Joyful Brethren newly risen from sleep,
his cap of feathers stolen from the Quetzal bird
enabled him to pipe the sun from the sky,
and pipe it back up. Yes, he was the tale-teller
who opened our eyes to the truth
of no truth. You could see how he moved crab-wise in daylight,
straight ahead in the dark, and in summer
how the rose on his belly bloomed
like the neon rose in the window of Big Joe's
Place where he drank his bar whiskey straight,
a gift from Joe's wife,
who trimmed his beard of red curls, carefully,
on Saturdays. Sundays he danced on the beach
trailed by a flock of gulls, a pack of children
at his heels, in his cavernous pockets food
whistled out of the town's pantrys. Believe,
he said, believe like a virgin
in perfection,
but keep an eye out for the blue horses, the knife
of the pardoner. The night he left town
he called back over his shoulder, God gives almonds
to some who have no teeth. That night

the minister decided to write of the almond
as a symbol of divine approval.
Men shouted down for their women who lingered
late in their kitchens.
Children grew old in their sleep.

The sea unsteadied the stars, as if
we were all part of the story.

from *Letters from the Coast*

Stephanie Hallgren

Prayer

When I was a girl, I was Sainte Genviève.
The clover beside the porch
was the heads of wounded
I'd bound in gauze.
Mother read on the lawn.
I blessed her with my baton
made from a wooden spoon
and a Christmas bulb.

Poor Mother. Where will you go
when the house burns down?
I wanted something tragic
and bright.
Wherever will we go, dear,
when we go wafting
char and hair
over the orchard?

Guilt is ashes, and like the peach tree
that floats its fruit toward my window,
renewed each summer. The secret purpose
of the sign of the cross
is to join the head and heart and arms,
to make a whole of what fails in each.

Marcia Hesselman

Butchering

He'd grab them by white feathered
necks — all gristle, cartilage, vertebrae
underneath — and as they
squawked, eyes bulging, he'd swing them dizzy
till the moment it all snapped;
string wound too tight on a button toy
rubber bands on balsa wood gliders
and pop —
head over the coop
body running aimlessly about the yard
stumbling over rocks as the cat watched
from her tree — all wide-eyed curiosity
at such easily captured lunch, her tail
a nervous flag.

That was the year Aunt Betty died
and Mother stopped talking — for a year
no sound, her laughter stilled, her voice
silenced, as she watched the holocaust in the yard.
And I never dreamed the chicks we'd brought
home, two at a time in paper bags
from the feed store; an Easter gift for every child,
I never dreamed we'd swing them like bolos,
fling scrawny bones about the yard
or that there I'd sit
dunking warm bird bodies in hot water tubs —
up, down, once, twice,
plucking feathers that smelled like chickens in
the rain —
too dumb to shelter in the coop
they'd stand gazing heavenward like
gawking tourists
devout buddhists, or the newly healed.

There they'd be; all beaks and beady eyes,
as rain poured down their gullets
drowning them where they stood
till I ran to hustle them in
sitting out the shower on straw
wet with feathers and shit,
the smell of feed pungent, sweet,
as they cackled, fought for perches,
settled down for the night —
till the weasel came,
clenched scrawny neck after neck
shook them hard, drug them warm and limp
back out the hole — feet prayer stiff —
till I grabbed the broom, waited one

night, waited 'cause he'd get hungry,
waited till he came
and he did, and I did and
no chickens that night
but one dead weasel, one dead sleek as
a seal body,
and that was the summer Aunt Betty died
and Mother stopped talking
and Dad and I butchered chickens.
In the yard that day, they trotted headless
about the grass, fell softly in the dust
and Mother watched,
her wordless eyes on the sky,
a steady gaze.

Susan Rawlins

What Is Important

In the commercial, young men
are killing fish. Around a campfire
they drink beer. The dead fish fry.
There are no women anywhere
in this story. *It just doesn't
get any better than this.*

My father writes odes to
slaughter: loving the animals,
you hunt; because you have
hunted, you kill. He brings home
their horns, their heads, their
skins, and writes of them.

I do not follow the logic,
but these are important ideas.

My father has learned a lot
lately and asks my opinion
before interrupting to tell me
the truth. With no interest
in words or people, he has
taken up writing. Two books
a year. Novels.

I have said what I have to say;
it has made no difference.

I have spent my life putting
words in rows "in the cause of
the small human heart, mine
especially." The flower that
favors me by blooming,
a hand's warmth, the comfort
of lunch, of clean white sheets.
Small things my mother taught me,
small loving things.

What I have learned lately is
not important, a better way
to clean glass. Small steps,
small increments. The goal is
a window so clean that
no one can see it.

Strasbourg in the Spring: A Guided Walk

Trust me when I tell you
to begin at the river Lill,
to walk the corridor of weeping
willows and dazzling chestnuts
with blooms erect as Christmas candles.
Follow its insinuations
toward the wooden footbridge and locks
announcing the old city.
Stop on the bridge and look back
to marvel how river, trees, and path
converge only where you stand.

Now you are ready to turn
toward the row of half-timbered
houses built right on the edge.
There you admire the window box pinks and blues
naive as weather and finally choose
the second house, the one with a brass
knocker shaped like the angel
of death. Touch her wing, her rib
if you must, but do not try to tip
the hourglass. Because no one answers,
you believe the house empty. Stepping inside,
you taste the warm loaf
cooling on the table. You are drawn
to the daguerreotype above the mantel.
Note how the face resembles yours.

Looking outside, you discover the sinking
sun has changed everything. When you decide
to let it go, turn into the dim hall.
You find your way to the back
bedroom and sit on the white coverlet.
Think of yourself as young,
a girl waving from a high window.
Now you notice a woman in a black
veil lying beside you. Ask her
if she remembers growing old.
When she does not answer,
tell her you have spent your life
searching for her. Then clasp
her hand, a perfect fit, and finally
admit you understand. Believe me
when I tell you I want nothing more.

Crossing The Connecticut

for Annalisa Cremin

The river lifts your hair
and draws it out around your face.
You wait, floating —
hands softly sculling,
your breasts, knees, toes barely breaking
the taut Connecticut.
We swim together, breastroking
the great bay above the dam
at Bellows Falls. The world's
rolled out like a dough of mirrors.
We move through the reflected
hills of New Hampshire,
the irregular shape of a white
farmhouse which breaks with our movement,
through space of domed sky
sliced by swifts
and swallows. Then north
along the reedy shore of Vermont —
our stomachs pale and flat,
sucked up above the darkly moving grasses.
We did not know about your illness then.
Chafed, blood rising to our cooling skins
we towelled each other. Laughed. Guessed
we'd gone two miles. I said, *We deserve*
every good thing that happens to us.
Oh, Lisa! My eyes fill
with the river. The swallows
make one last turn,
dip their wings
and rise.

Waterfront Photo

Even if the seine fleet wasn't in
or our pale arms weren't sleeveless
I could tell where we were; which
summer from our past
by the size of your hands
swollen from three months work
rebuilding a cannery and dock
constructed first back in 1912.

Years ago
when men did not drive to work
inside but killed animals for food; dug
rows in the mud for seed, their hands
adjusted slowly like pekoe sun tea
to the color of rich earth. New skin
grew right over the dirt.

There are men in the city, men
right here in our small town
whose hands are smooth
knickless as a slab of marble.
Hands perfect and really quite pink.
I study such things
like how your callouses grow thickest
where your fingers meet the palm
and when cut draw no blood.

And there are men, musicians
maybe or lawyers
able to grab at small objects
with the tips of their fingers
instead of rolling one hand on its side
and letting the thumb do the work. Men
who can sit next to a woman
in a library or church
rubbing her legs covered in nylon
without being heard
or lay in the dark with her
on a sleeping bag
unzipped and opened flat
with hands that prowl easily
without catching on each lofty seam.

There are even men
so unlike yourself
who would drive a bent nail
deeper into the grain of mahogany
or even teak
just to get the job done.

Rebecca Seiferle

Slaughtering Goats at Eastertime

The bucks butt each other out of the gate.
We kill them because their sex
snaps 2X4's, leaps any fence,
smells of rotten cheese.
Bordering backyards with their lust,
they are better dead than someone's pet,
a castrated weed-eater on a chain.
But it is hard to kill them
when they come for milk,
caprine-cute, speckle-eared, wagging
their tails like puppies. They smell
of alfalfa hay and mother worry,
of midnight crooning to a laboring doe,
of pedigree ink and mating season,
of the one that died in the snow,
of the one we carried into the house.
Their sun-colored coats, their gentle manners,
their stunning leaps, the way they cavort
in morning, shame our stuttering alleluias.
Three times a day we fed them bottles.
Now they follow us like our own children
into the killing pen.

DIANE WALD's poems have been published in many journals, including *American Poetry Review* and *The Massachusetts Quarterly*. A graduate of the University of Massachusetts, she lives in Jamaica Plains, Massachusetts.

CAROL KYLE, Urbana, Illinois, teaches at the University of Illinois. Recent publications include poems in *River Styx* and the *English Journal*.

LINNEA JOHNSON is a member of the English Department at Muhlenberg College in Allentown, Pennsylvania.

ROBERT CRUM resides in Somerville, Massachusetts.

REBECCA McCLANAHAN DEVIT is a writer in Charlotte, North Carolina.

HELEN ELLIS is a professor at Greenfield Community College and lives in Bernardston, Massachusetts. Her publications include three books and several poems and short stories.

BARBARA HORTON, Evanston, Illinois, is currently an advertising copywriter with McDougal, Little & Company. Her poetry has been published in *Kansas Quarterly* and *Plainsong*.

CYNTHIA HUNTINGTON has published a book, *The Fish-Wife*, and resides in Huntington Beach, California. She teaches poetry at the University of California at Irvine.

MARY CHRIS LECHE lives in Lafayette, Louisiana.

JAMES MAGORIAN's recently published poems can be found in *Open Places* and *Plainsong*. He presently lives in Lincoln, Nebraska.

LILLIAN ROBINSON resides in Oley, Pennsylvania.

PETER SEARS, Portland, Oregon, works at the Oregon Arts Commission. His chapbooks include *Bike Run* and *I Want to Be a Crowd*.

BARBARA WINDER is a member of the English Department at Western Connecticut State University. Her work has appeared in many periodicals and anthologies.

SUSAN FAWCETT, New York, is the author of two college writing textbooks. Her poetry has appeared in *The Nation, Ms.*, and *Poetry Review.*

MARGARET BENBOW of Portage, Wisconsin, was second place winner in 1986, and received honorable mention in 1985. Her work has appeared in *Poetry*, the *Antioch Review*, and various literary journals.

RHEA COHEN is a frequent poetry reader in Washington, D.C. Her work has been published in many anthologies and journals.

CHARLES ATKINSON is a writer in Santa Cruz, California.

MELISSA CANNON, Nashville, Tennessee, was winner of the 1986 Croton Review Award in Poetry. Her poetry has been published most recently in *HomeWords: A Book of Tennessee Writers.*

REGINA DECORMIER-SHEKERJIAN's recent work was included in *The Hungry Poet's Cookbook, Kansas Quarterly*, and *The Massachusetts Review*. She lives in New Paltz, New York.

STEPHANIE HALLGREN currently resides in Honolulu, Hawaii. Her recent work appears in *Black Warrior Review, North Dakota Quarterly*, and a variety of other journals.

MARCIA HESSELMAN, Kokomo, Indiana, teaches writing at Indiana University. She has been published in *Jazz Street* and *Great Lakes Review*, and she was second place winner of the 1985 Wisconsin Fellowship of Poets Prize.

SUSAN RAWLINS' work has appeared in the *San Francisco Chronicle* and the *Christian Science Monitor*. She teaches writing at San Francisco State University and lives in Berkeley, California.

PAULETTE ROESKE, Evanston, Illinois, has had work appear in several magazines and anthologies and was first place winner in the Illinois Writers New Broadsides Competition. She is a teacher at College of Lake County in Grayslake, Illinois.

MARGARET SANDS is a writer in Walpole, New Hampshire.

MARY LOU SANELLI, Port Townsend, Washington, runs a dance studio and teaches modern jazz. Her poetry has appeared in *Poetry Seattle* and *Northwest Magazine.*

REBECCA SEIFERLE's work has been published in *Women's Quarterly Review, Carolina Quarterly*, and *Negative Capability*. She resides in Bloomfield, New Mexico.

Typography by Electronic Imaging, Incorporated, Champaign, Illinois.
Printing by Crouse Printing, Champaign, Illinois.
Front cover photo by Raymond Bial, Urbana, Illinois.

.